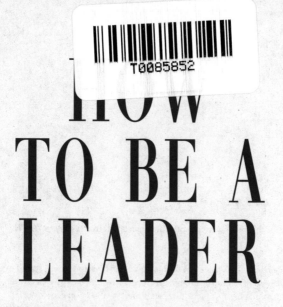

HOW TO BE A LEADER

15 MINUTES A DAY TO ESTABLISH COMMUNICATION, RESILIENCY, CREATIVITY, AND HUMILITY

David M. Cote

HarperCollins
LEADERSHIP

AN IMPRINT OF HarperCollins

Portions of this book were adapted and excerpted from *Winning Now, Winning Later*.

Published by HarperCollins Leadership, an imprint of HarperCollins Focus LLC.

Any internet addresses, phone numbers, or company or product information printed in this book are offered as a resource and are not intended in any way to be or to imply an endorsement by HarperCollins Leadership, nor does HarperCollins Leadership vouch for the existence, content, or services of these sites, phone numbers, companies, or products beyond the life of this book.

ISBN 978-1-4003-4386-7 (eBook)
ISBN 978-1-4003-4385-0 (paperback)

Library of Congress Cataloging-in-Publication Data on File

Printed in the United States of America
24 25 26 27 28 LBC 5 4 3 2 1

S trong leadership is crucial. Yet one in four leaders indicates that leadership development is either nonexistent or low quality in their organization.[1] Sixty-nine percent of employees say they would work harder if they felt their efforts were better recognized by management and other leaders.[2]

Leadership matters—it really does. And the trick, as I like to say, is in the doing. On a daily operational level, you have to dedicate yourself to actually doing it, pushing yourself and others on your team and in your organization to go beyond what they think is possible, every small step of the way. To perform well today while investing in tomorrow, your business must do what everyone else claims to be doing. And that will only happen if you as the leader demand it at the outset and accept no compromises.

Natural leaders are a finite group of people. To become a leader, you must be willing to cultivate your talent (using strengths and weaknesses) into high-quality leadership. You must push your people to do two seemingly conflicting things at the same time. Rest assured, your people have it in them to deliver, so long as you provide diligent encouragement, guidance, and oversight along the way, while also making sure you have the right people in the right positions. When providing guidance, you must do more than just say, "Do better." You're responsible for providing thought starters or suggestions that will mobilize your people to think differently about the issues at hand.

This book is a guide to help you become a true leader. No matter what size your team or business is, *How to Be a Leader* will teach you how to pursue goals, commit to change, inspire others, create alignment, improve productivity, manage different opinions, create a connected culture, and build a presence that goes beyond a standard nine-to-five.

Each day you will focus on a leadership topic while using the prompts as a springboard for change within your leadership style and business development. I will share experiences from my time as CEO of Honeywell, but I'll also include stories of my beginnings as a factory worker. I know what it means to truly work your way up. I hope you will find value in my shared experiences and advice so you can become a better leader.

YOU CAN DO BETTER

When I graduated from high school in 1970, I was lazy, immature, and directionless—anxious to get going in life (whatever that meant) but lacking any idea where or how. I was admitted to the University of New Hampshire, but initially declined to go, opting instead to work at my father's garage and later with my uncle in Michigan as a carpenter. However, none of that worked out, so the following year I enrolled at the university. Instead of going to class over the next couple of years, I drank, smoked, and played cards. At the end of my sophomore year, the assistant dean of students said I could no longer live on campus because I was a troublemaker.

The next year, as I continued with my studies, I took a night job running a punch press at the General Electric plant in Hooksett, New Hampshire. A friend and I also bought a thirty-three-foot, seventeen-year-old fishing boat, intending to start our own business as commercial fishermen in York Harbor, Maine. It was a lot to handle, and something had to give. So I stopped attending classes entirely and earned a 1.8 grade point average. I quit a second time, determined to become rich as a fisherman while working nights at General Electric. Fishing was a lot more fun than sitting in class. Eventually my buddy got married, we sold the boat, and I married my girlfriend.

It was April 1975, and my wife and I lived in a third-floor, unheated, uninsulated apartment in New Hampshire, taking it a day at a time with no plans for the future. A month after our wedding, my wife was pregnant. A couple of months after that, she told me she couldn't work any longer because of the pregnancy. It was on me to provide for the three of us.

I was terrified. We had only a hundred dollars in the bank. When I did the math, I learned that we were spending two dollars more each week than my job paid. In less than a year, assuming we stuck to a bare-bones budget, we would go broke, if we didn't freeze first. In our apartment, the only heat came in from the units below us and a blower off the gas stove.

I had to get serious about my life—our survival depended on it. I needed a better paying job, and that meant I would have to finish college. So I did that, attending college during the day while continuing to work nights at General Electric. My entire life changed overnight. I quit smoking cigarettes and started exercising. I became more diligent as an employee. I stopped wasting my suddenly scarce time and focused on school.

My son, Ryan, was born on February 24, 1976. I still remember sealing the window cracks with masking tape to reduce the draft, looking at him bundled up against the cold in his crib, and fearing I'd never be able to take care of him. I graduated college in May 1976. About six weeks later, I applied for and received my first salaried job, as an internal auditor at the General Electric Aircraft Engines business.

I share this story to illustrate a simple but underappreciated fact: individuals and groups can push themselves much further than they think.

———◇———

What is preventing you from making the changes you know will make you a more effective leader?

What can you use as motivation to inspire change for yourself?

YOU MUST PURSUE LONG-
AND SHORT-TERM GOALS

L eaders might value broader objectives like sustainability, competitiveness, and growth, and wax eloquent about their commitment to these long-term goals, but when called upon to allocate scarce resources, they focus on the current year's plan and do what it takes to meet their numbers. In their view, they have no choice—their job depends on pleasing bosses and shareholders *today*, not tomorrow.

The notion that there is no way to pursue long- and short-term goals at the same time, and therefore leaders have no choice but to embrace short-termism, is one of the most pernicious beliefs circulating in business today. A McKinsey study found that firms that followed long-term strategies amassed $7 billion more in market capitalization between 2001 and 2014, and generated 47 percent more revenue growth and 36 percent more earnings growth, on average, than companies that took a shorter-term approach.[3] Nevertheless, as one 2014 study found, two-thirds of executives and directors reported that "pressure for short-term results had increased over the previous five years."[4] Short-termism has become so rampant that influential leaders are speaking out against it, with some advocating that we relax the reporting requirements on public firms so that leaders don't feel such intense and constant pressure to make their numbers.

We can't regulate our way to long-termism—the problem is too complex and deeply entrenched. Instead, we need a comprehensive mindset shift on the part of leaders and managers at every level. Somehow, we've convinced ourselves that we can invest in the future only if we let short-term performance tank. But that's not true. Strong short- and long-term performance only *seem* mutually exclusive. As a leader, you can and must pursue both at the same time. Unless you do, you and your team or organization will never reach your full potential.

I believe you can pursue short- and long-term goals if you follow three principles. Read through these principles and determine how you can apply them to your business.

Three Principles of Short- and Long-Term Performance

1. Scrub accounting and business practices down to what is real.
2. Invest in the future, but not excessively.
3. Grow while keeping fixed costs constant.

---◇---

Are you thinking about both the short-term and long-term in your plans?

How do you ensure your short-term actions are consistent with your long-term goals?

COMMIT TO "BLUE BOOK" SESSIONS

B lue book" sessions began with a blue-covered notebook and designated time I set aside to hold myself accountable. I wanted to make a habit of carving out time to sit by myself, put aside the daily pressures of my job, and just *think* about the company. During one of these sessions, I challenged myself to identify steps I needed to take to put Honeywell on a better path. As I sat there pondering, it came to me that I would have to find a way to invest in new products, services, process improvement, geographical expansion, and so on. But given investors' low opinion of me, I also had to deliver something for them in the short term—otherwise, I wouldn't survive. I couldn't push investment off to some unspecified future date, and I also couldn't invest to such an extent that we once again fell short of shareholder expectations. We would have to do both at the same time.

Further, I realized we *could* do both at the same time. Short- and long-term goals were more tightly intertwined than they appeared. By taking the right actions to improve operations now, we could position ourselves to improve performance later, while the reverse would also hold true: short-term results would validate that we were on the right long-term path.

———◇———

Buy a notebook that's dedicated for your own blue book sessions.

Plan a recurring blue book meeting with yourself. Block off the time on your work calendar so no one schedules another meeting. Commit to at least one blue book session a month.

ADOPT AN INTELLECTUAL MINDSET

Fundamentally, preparing for both the short and long term isn't about changing specific processes, policies, or strategies, but rather about adopting a different, more intellectual mindset. Planting seeds for the future while also achieving short-term results is much harder to pull off than just aiming for one of these goals exclusively. It's so difficult, in fact, that many executives and managers throw up their hands in defeat. Absolving themselves of any responsibility to achieve both short- and long-term goals, they shrink from asking tough questions and actively shield themselves and others from probing too deeply. Instead of finding new ways to support innovation and investment while achieving short-term goals, they fall back on the same old strategies, policies, and procedures, relying on accounting sleight of hand to make it all work.

Don't let this be you. You *can* achieve short- and long-term goals simultaneously, but that means you will need to puzzle it out, quarter after quarter, year after year. Challenge yourself, your team, and your organization to think more about customers, markets, and processes than you previously have. Cultivate a mindset of analytic rigor and attention to detail. Ask challenging questions of yourself and others, and dig until you've uncovered satisfying answers, even if that means acknowledging difficult truths. Decide right now to become a serious, engaged, and honest scholar of your business instead of a passive overseer of it.

How can you use facts and analytics to make better decisions for your business?

Make a list of reports that will help you monitor these decisions and accomplish short- and long-term goals.

STOP DOING THE SAME THING OVER AND OVER

When I served as CFO at a General Electric business, we tried to reduce the amount of capital we deployed in operating our businesses, and in line with that goal, my boss had decided that our business unit needed to reduce the $1 billion in inventory we maintained—and I was going to lead the charge. The assignment caught me by surprise—I wasn't sure how to proceed. I had seen other businesses flounder when pursuing such initiatives. The boss would decree that henceforth the company would keep only a certain amount of inventory on hand to shrink the amount of cash it had locked up. Months later, inventory levels would creep back up, and the amount of cash locked up would increase as well—*again*.

I wanted to try a new approach, but I didn't know what that would be. We convened a cross-functional team and asked them: Why *did* inventory reduction initiatives usually fail? What can we do differently?

"If we're going to fail," I said, "let's at least do it differently. The definition of *insanity* is doing the same thing over and over, always expecting a different result."

One manufacturing leader identified dissatisfied customers as the reason why these initiatives usually failed. Once a business reduced inventory, customer delivery usually suffered because we didn't have the items we needed in stock. Customers complained, and the sales force applied pressure on the business to stock more product. Eventually inventory levels were right back where they had been. Inventory levels and customer satisfaction were directly related. You could have lower inventory levels or high customer satisfaction, but not both.

We wondered if we could find a way to reduce inventory levels *while also* keeping our products readily available and ready to ship so that customer satisfaction wouldn't plummet. My team and I spent an entire day puzzling over it and decided to assess our entire process. Running an analysis, we found that it took eighteen weeks end to end. That seemed like an extraordinarily long time. What if we could render the whole process more efficient, shrinking our "cycle time," as we called it, down to a couple of days? We'd be able to reduce warehouse inventory while still providing great customer service because we'd be able to replenish our stock much more quickly. The dramatically improved efficiency would also help us reduce a lot of operational cost.

Our team began working on improving our processes to reduce

cycle time in forecasting, supply chain, production, and distribution. We began providing immediate feedback to plants on what had shipped that day, shortening supplier lead times, dramatically reducing lot sizes (the quantity of a product model we made during a given production run), and reducing transportation time to warehouses. Over a four-year period, these ongoing efforts reduced cycle time to about two weeks. We were able to cut inventory levels in half, while also improving our on-time delivery rate by almost 10 percent. Instead of focusing on just one goal, we had prompted ourselves to think about our business as a whole, and to pose questions nobody had asked before. The improved process could sustain gains across a range of metrics over time.

---◇---

Is there a process within your business that others have suggested analyzing and performing differently?

What is the biggest complaint you receive from customers? Commit to brainstorming with your team on ways you can resolve the issue.

Where do you see conflicting goals that could benefit from better understanding root causes?

NO MORE LAME PRESENTATIONS

S trategic planning is essential for every business. In most businesses, there is a certain time of the year when departments (or
businesses) meet to discuss goals, updates on progress and sales, and
accomplishments. Sometimes these presentations are just a word
salad with no real substance.

Each July at Honeywell our businesses presented findings and
plans to the CEO, with similar presentations taking place down
through the ranks. These presentations were, in a word, *bullshit*.
Leaders had no clue how they would run their businesses over the
next five years, what big initiatives they would have to push to make
their goals, or what changes in their industry they should anticipate, or better, lead. Rather than choosing goals intentionally, they
picked ambitious targets they thought would please their bosses,
without regard for whether the business could realistically achieve
them. They might have factored in the benefit of downsizing, the
introduction of new products or services, process improvement, or
other cost-savings initiatives, but then didn't include as an expense

the funds to bankroll these initiatives because it would depress the outlook. To cover themselves, they threw around lofty language and piled on hundreds of pages of charts and tables, hoping to look smart. Without much critical analysis, leaders gave their blessings, leaving the businesses to go execute whatever they wanted without follow-up or accountability. "Strategy," such as it was, had no relevance. Operational considerations and making the quarter became daily concerns, with strategy fading to the background. As a leader, you must eradicate the BS and reinvent planning.

When leaders pretend they know more than they do, call them on it. When a team would regale me with long lists of "competitive strengths," this was a red flag. A strong business is lucky to enjoy a couple of key advantages over its peers.

Once you and the other leaders at your business begin analyzing proposed strategic plans critically, your plans will become sharper, more realistic, and more successful.

---♦---

Is your planning process more of an annual event rather than a rigorous, ongoing examination of your strategy?

Do you have Growth Days set aside for periodic review of progress on strategic goals?

STOP INTELLECTUAL LAZINESS

When I arrived at Honeywell, I stepped into an organization utterly unused to probing for root causes to problems and to advancing new and creative solutions. Executives and managers pursued goals along a single dimension, doing whatever it took to make their numbers in the current quarter without concern for their actions' broader consequences. Leaders never pushed themselves to develop the kind of new and interesting solutions that would permanently change their businesses for the better and achieve multiple goals at once.

Inevitably, such intellectual laziness coarsened the level of discourse that existed day-to-day. Many businesses lacked any drive to think deeply about their businesses, and unchallenged by leadership to do so, teams held meetings that were essentially useless, their presentations clogged with feel-good jargon, meaningless numbers, and analytic frameworks whose chief purpose was to hide faulty logic and make the business look good. When you did a bit of digging, you found that most executives and managers didn't understand their businesses very well, if at all.

Certainly they didn't understand their customers. I'll never forget a trip I took early on in my tenure to an air show to visit with a customer of our Aerospace unit. The team had briefed me on the visit, and I had gone into the meeting, along with the leader of the business unit, his product manager, and the salesperson, thinking we would discuss a great new product we had. As is my practice, I kicked off the conversation by asking if Honeywell was meeting their expectations. "I'm glad you stopped by," the customer CEO said, "because we have just about finalized the lawsuit we are filing against you for nonperformance on our development project." What!? My colleagues looked at one another and at me in shock—none of us had known how angry this customer was. We had lacked the slightest bit of insight into how our customers were experiencing their relationship with us. I begged for time, and with a bit of scrambling on our part we were able to prevent the lawsuit from materializing.

But it wasn't just this team, and it wasn't just customers. Leaders at Honeywell hadn't studied their operational processes in any depth. They didn't understand the fundamentals of their technologies, their markets, or their business cycles. They didn't know their supply chains. They weren't in touch with how rank-and-file employees viewed the business. And they didn't understand key liabilities, such as the environmental lawsuits we faced.

———◇———

What new and interesting solutions could permanently change your businesses for the better and achieve multiple goals at once? Bring your team together and ask them the same question. Provide ample time and resources to assist in the thought process.

Do you really understand what your customers think about your business performance for them?

LEADERSHIP FRAMEWORK

M y first and most enduring challenge as CEO was to dramatically improve the quality of both our individual thinking and our group discussions. To convey how I did that, let me introduce a leadership framework I have long used. As I see it, leadership boils down to three distinct tasks. First, leaders must know how to mobilize a large group of people. Second, they must pick the right direction toward which their team or organization should move. And third, they must get the entire team or organization moving in that direction to execute against that designated goal. Most people associate leadership disproportionately with the first element: inspiring the group. They think of charismatic leaders like Steve Jobs delivering lofty speeches that blow people away and motivate them to perform. In truth, mobilizing people is only about 5 percent of the leader's job. The best leaders dedicate almost all their time to the latter two elements: making great decisions and executing consistently with those decisions.

To remedy this problem, I spent a great deal of time defining what it meant to make decisions in an honest, informed, deliberate way. The first and best way to do that, I realized, was to model the process of critical inquiry myself. I'd make it clear that, yes, we *were* going to push ourselves to achieve two conflicting goals at the same time. But rather than simply dictate these goals, I'd start team members down the path to making a sound decision, asking them critical questions about their businesses and prompting them to generate creative solutions.

Leaders must be demanding of their people, otherwise they'll achieve only marginal results. At the same time, leaders don't have to be nasty about it. I always tried to pose my questions courteously, remembering how as an employee I responded better when leaders showed me respect rather than telling me that I was wrong or barking out an order.

———◇———

Think of a leader you didn't like. What specifically bothered you, and how do you ensure you don't do the same things? How did their actions impact your leadership style?

What critical questions can you ask team members to guide them to generate creative solutions?

PLANNING FOR THE LONG-TERM

I pushed leaders to think more deeply about the complex, long-term picture in every decision they faced. Further, I challenged them to think carefully about what might go wrong. It's so easy to discount low-probability events in decision-making, even though these events might prove disastrous if they do occur. By considering the downside more aggressively, our teams often illuminated important issues we might otherwise have missed.

In challenging other leaders intellectually, I strove specifically to push them beyond the incrementalism that usually exists inside organizations—the tendency to consider the short-term implications of a decision exclusively and to ignore the long term. When leaders were thinking of adding capacity to an existing high-cost plant, I would ask them why they hadn't considered establishing a new presence in a low-cost, high-quality location. "Well," they said, "it's less expensive to simply build on to our existing plant." Taking this particular short-term business situation in isolation, that might have been true. But when you considered how establishing a new presence elsewhere might pave the way for future expansion, it might have made more sense to pay a little more now and build in a potentially lucrative new market.

Likewise, when leaders assessed which parts of their business were core and which were susceptible to outsourcing, they tended at first to regard 95 percent of operations as core. When we explored it further, we found they defined some operational areas that way simply because they believed it was too expensive for the company to outsource those areas. They failed to consider the broader, long-term picture: the cost of managing these parts of the business, the physical buildings required, the reduction in our ability to adapt to economic change, the cost of continuing to invest in these parts, and so on. Factor in these hidden, long-term implications, and the cost equation often looked very different, making it far more desirable to outsource these supposedly core areas. (In my experience, organizations can generally outsource between 30 and 70 percent of what they do.)

———◇———

Assess your business. What percentage is core and what percentage could be outsourced? What areas can you think of in your business where decisions that look smart for the short term aren't so smart when viewed for the long term?

Is there a long-term goal you and other leaders have discussed and ultimately turned down? Should you reconsider or reassess the goal's structure and plan? Could the outcome of the long-term goal drastically change the business's future?

TAKE YOUR THREE MINUTES

While reading a book about the construction of the Panama Canal, I came across an anecdote about the project's chief engineer, whose math teacher used to say, "If you have five minutes to solve a problem, use the first three to figure out how you're going to do it." I repeated this story within Honeywell in an effort to get people to slow down and think about problems a bit more. On one occasion, leaders of our Aerospace business unit were considering whether to proceed with a possible acquisition. At the end of the meeting I asked the team if they really wanted to go ahead with the deal and if they could guarantee the results. Most of the team said yes right away, but the head of Aerospace at the time, Tim Mahoney, said, "I'd like to take my three minutes. Can I get back to you Monday?" I loved that response and readily agreed.

Tim pored through the details of the deal yet again, taking the time to identify additional opportunities, and decided to proceed. We spent $600 million acquiring that company. About five months after the deal closed, Tim's team landed a $2.4 billion order we hadn't included when valuing the company. That extra three minutes really paid off!

Next time you encounter a problem, vow to take three minutes to thoroughly think through the details. Make a list if you need to and slow down.

PUSHING OTHERS MEANS PUSHING YOURSELF

A sking your leaders to make decisions in a more rigorous way means you have to put in more work. You should spend time in advance of meetings generating key questions for teams, and stay on the people involved, as well as broader trends affecting the business. During my fifteen years as CEO, I traveled to plants and customers in about a hundred countries to better understand our operations and the challenges they faced. Back at our headquarters, I read five newspapers a day as well as key business publications and books and magazines on a wide range of topics. I met with a variety of people—CEOs from outside our industry, financial types, investors, policymakers—to understand how they were thinking about emerging trends. I also spent time during my blue book sessions sitting alone in my office thinking about our businesses. I posed questions to myself and tried to answer them, and I reflected on external trends affecting our markets, pondering how our businesses might have to adapt.

In keeping myself informed, I took it upon myself to develop a certain amount of functional expertise. I would read up on diverse subjects, such as information technology (IT), law, and social media. I knew trends in these areas were affecting our businesses, so I wanted to be able to talk about them. I hardly became an expert, but the questions I asked prompted team members who were experts to think in new and creative ways. Because they knew I'd be asking hard-hitting questions, they had to be ready to explain their business ideas to me in simple ways that even a layperson could understand—an exercise that forced them to refine their thinking. Simplicity and concision are tough. If you can't convey a thought clearly and in a few words, then your comprehension of the topic is probably lacking.

My efforts to inform myself in diverse fields prompted nonexperts on our teams to read up on them as well. If the gray-haired CEO knew enough about the Internet of Things (IoT), say, to be dangerous, our senior executives in legal, human resources, or operations needed to as well. Otherwise they would risk looking uninformed during our conversations.

Commit to learn more about the business you are leading. Check out books from the library, read articles written by qualified experts, and listen to relative podcasts. Keep a notepad and jot down questions you need answered. These are questions you can ask your team or research yourself.

ALIGN YOUR ORGANIZATION AROUND THE STRATEGY

Informed decision-making is one thing, but it's not enough. Just because a leader makes a decision doesn't mean anything will happen. To achieve long- and short-term objectives at the same time—or any other two seemingly conflicting goals—leaders also have to take a rigorous and informed approach to execution. Leaders often believe they shouldn't try to micromanage the business. As they see it, people further down in the organization need a sense of autonomy in order to thrive, so leaders should delegate and get out of the way.

Delegation and trust are indeed vital—you can't do everything yourself, and you shouldn't try. That said, you don't want delegation to verge into a total abdication of authority on your part. You must verify that employees and the organization are actually executing as they are supposed to. I learned this lesson the hard way when

I served as vice president of General Electric's consumer service division, which fixed the company's appliances for customers. The business was sizable but demand was decreasing because of improving product quality (people didn't need to repair their dishwashers or washing machines as often), and our labor costs were too high. To improve the business, I embarked on a restructuring plan (a decision I made thanks to numerous field visits with customers, service technicians, and others). I also invested heavily in a big IT project to improve how we scheduled our service technicians. Once in place, this project would significantly boost customer service while reducing our costs.

Since I didn't know much about IT, I relied on our IT leader to keep me informed on how the project was going. Everything seemed fine—until one day, when the project blew up. It became clear that the system wasn't going to work. What a disaster. Ever since, I made a practice of keeping far closer tabs on important projects.

The idea that as a leader you can focus on strategy and delegate its implementation to great people is a fallacy. Time is limited, and faced with urgent priorities, even the most talented people will let difficult, longer-term projects slide. Leaders must get out in the field to confirm that these projects are actually happening. They also must make sure the "machinery" works every day—that employees have the tools and processes they need to execute their decisions, and further, that they're working hard to improve these tools and processes.

———◇———

Do you engage with managers to get their opinions on key business issues? If not, make it a priority to do this and set up a routine check-in.

Do you query team members about how they are executing on projects and how things could be better? If not, make it a priority to do this and take their feedback into consideration.

Do you visit the field to see what's really happening? If not, get started.

YOU ARE A PERFORMANCE COACH

Executing the right leadership plan isn't just about holding people accountable. By asking insightful questions, you will also serve your leaders as a performance coach, keeping them focused on operations and giving them an intellectual framework they can use to solve specific problems. It's easy for a leader to say, "We need some new products. Here's some money. Go do it." But think of the benefit when a leader challenges people to think about *how* they're going to innovate so that they don't just fund a bunch of screwball projects. How will they set up ideation to ensure that lots of good ideas are generated? How will they determine which new product ideas to fund and which to jettison? Who will they assign to product development so that the organization takes it seriously? What will they do to ensure that technologists are interacting with the marketing team so that the market actually wants these new products?

How will they understand the user, installer, and maintainer experience? Will a product manager own the product or service from the beginning to ensure that the introduction doesn't get bogged down?

When I posed similar questions to team members, I was giving leaders the benefit of my experience, alerting them to the kinds of operational issues they would likely encounter when undertaking specific projects. I had developed a practice of asking questions in various situations as they arose so as to avoid my previous mistakes. By posing these questions to team members rather than providing easy answers, I helped them understand their business better and put them in a position to execute, leaving it to them to come up with answers that would work in their specific situations. Hopefully, the time and effort I spent would increase the odds that team members would succeed.

———◇———

Do you help your people think through an issue or do you just provide an answer? Write down five to ten questions you could pose to your team members. Reflect on your own successes and failures, so you can develop questions that also include your previous experience.

TIGHTEN UP YOUR METRICS

Many people will say what gets measured gets done, but that's not necessarily true. If you measure something, the metric will get better, but the underlying performance might not improve at all. People will do whatever it takes to get the metric where it needs to be, losing sight of the business intent underlying the goal. It becomes "compliance with words," as I like to say, not "compliance with intent."

As a leader, you shouldn't take performance as indicated by the metrics for granted. It is important to review operations rigorously to make sure improvements in metrics reflects real improvements in the underlying processes. Often leadership places balancing metrics to ensure that one metric didn't improve at the expense of other, critical parts of the business. In reducing the cost of functions like finance, IT, legal, or HR, you don't want the support those functions provided across the organization to be compromised. At

Honeywell, we conducted anonymous internal surveys to determine if customer service from those areas was improving.

Not infrequently, our insistence on rigorous metrics led to significant improvements. For years we had tried but failed to improve the diversity of our workforce. Part of the problem was that we were forging policy at headquarters with only a limited knowledge of our workforce in local facilities. To remedy the situation, we created a sophisticated tool that combined our own data with data from the Department of Labor. The tool allowed us to track the availability of talent in local areas by job code, broken down by ethnicity and gender. Using this tool, we could compare diversity levels in particular plants and even in particular teams to the diversity in local talent pools. That allowed us to challenge managers who claimed, for one reason or another, they didn't have access to well-qualified, diverse talent.

We also began to measure the opportunities a leader had to improve diversity by tracking what happened with new hires and with attrition. Were leaders doing enough to recruit and retain diverse talent who had come on board? Every leader reported on his or her progress in this area twice annually to myself and my staff. As a result, we made steady progress year after year, rather than simply maintaining the status quo.

I've always said, "The trick is in the doing." It was great to make smart, informed decisions, but the real substance of any decision is getting it done. Leaders everywhere have more or less the same knowledge. They read the same books and periodicals. They talk to the same people. They have access to the same consultants. To gain an advantage, you must perform better, and that means understanding your operations better, looking for ways to improve, and putting those improvements in place. Leaders can't stand on the sidelines. They have to get out there in the field, immerse themselves in what their teams are doing, monitor progress, and hold people accountable. Then they have to use all of that knowledge they amassed to help inform their decision-making going forward.

What are you planning on measuring in your business?

What can you do in your performance to make sure operations within your company don't shift elsewhere?

START SCHEDULING "X" DAYS

You might find the prospect of modeling intellectual rigor for your team or organization daunting. How do you do it with so many demands on your time? For starters, I heartily recommend you dedicate time each month to learning about your business(es) and engaging in unstructured thinking. It's hard to think, read, and learn when endless meetings clog up your day. I developed a practice of sitting down with my calendar at the beginning of each fiscal year and asking my assistants to designate two or three days each month as "X" days, during which they wouldn't schedule any meetings. I'd spend some of those days alone thinking about our businesses. On other X days I'd make impromptu trips to learn about our businesses or pay a surprise visit to a facility. I'd also designate twelve additional days as "growth days," holding intensive sessions with leadership teams to help them think through various growth or operations initiatives. My staff had to hold these growth days on their calendars as well so that we didn't have to reconcile our calendars in the event we wanted to schedule a meeting (team members got these days back to use as they pleased if we wound up not holding a meeting that included them). Sometimes I had to schedule meetings on an X day, but anticipating that this would happen, I set aside more of these days at the beginning of the year than needed.

On my regularly scheduled days, I made sure to free up as much time and mind-space as I could for thinking. If you haven't gotten serious about tightening up your calendar, now is the time to start. Do you really need all those meetings? Are there ways to minimize the length of essential meetings and still make progress? I am not against meetings—they are essential for leaders, not least because they help us bring facts to the surface and generate good ideas. At the same time, so many meetings are excessively long, unnecessary, and inconclusive. One of my favorite techniques is to require that teams provide me with a summary page at the beginning of the meeting or beforehand so that I can get the gist of the issue up front as well as the team's recommendations.

———◊———

How much time do you *really* spend thinking? Do you organize your calendar to ensure that you have blocked out enough time, or are you a victim of your calendar?

MEETINGS & NOTES

To minimize the number of follow-up meetings required to resolve issues, and thus maximize the time on your calendar for thinking, I recommend ending every meeting by establishing the who, what, and when of any follow-up actions. Just because a team reaches consensus on an issue doesn't mean a decision will actually be implemented. Be clear what the follow-up action is, and when it comes to the "who," never accept "the team" as an answer. You want the name of someone who will ensure the required work gets done. On "when," remember Parkinson's law, which says that work expands to fill the time allotted. Don't be afraid to create tight timelines, because sometimes the culture demands them.

Also be sure to make the most of your unstructured hours between meetings. A great technique to try is what I call "bring-up notes." In their capacity as managers, most leaders keep track of all the deliverables people owe them and when. Rather than waste mental energy thinking about all that, I wrote down each deliverable and the due date on a separate piece of paper at the end of a meeting and had my assistant file it. Every day she handed me "bring-up notes" for items that had been due the day before. If I had already received the deliverable, I tore up the note. If I hadn't, I started inquiring about when I'd receive it. With bring-up notes, I was able to keep everyone accountable, allowing myself more time, energy, and mental space to read and think. Bear in mind, this began in an era before smartphones. These days productivity apps and other software can serve a similar function for you, especially if you don't have an assistant.

———————◇———————

Are you using meetings as opportunities to debate pressing issues in a rigorous way?

Do you just bark an order, or do you take the time to run people through a series of questions to help structure their thinking? Do you push others to articulate their ideas and the logic behind them and reserve your opinions until the end?

FEWER LEADERS

I t is important not to have too many leaders. Too often organizations suffer from a kind of "leadership bloat." They establish new leadership positions in order to lend significance to exciting new business initiatives, but they don't do enough to ensure that their existing leaders are working as efficiently as possible. The result—too many leaders—drags down performance, even if the vast majority of those leaders are high performers. That's because more leaders equals more bureaucracy.

Leaders don't just lead—they create work for other people, in the form of meetings, sign-offs, projects, procedures, priorities, and so on, especially if they're good leaders. Others in the organization then spend more of their time responding to these leaders and less time leading or managing their own team members. Each leader has their own staff—adding yet more cost and complexity to the organization. And when you have more leaders, you have more slots you need to fill as people retire or leave the organization. With a bit of effort, you can motivate your leaders to operate more efficiently—thus eliminating the "need" for additional leadership.

Does your organization have too many leaders?

When leaders depart, do you stop to ask whether you really need anyone in that position? Can you combine that position with another one?

When a staff member wants a new leadership position in order to focus on an initiative (oftentimes warranted), do you push them to cut a leadership position elsewhere?

QUESTION YOURSELF

I t's important, especially as you rise in seniority, to make sure you're not just always thinking, but are constantly questioning your own decisions. In public, you have to convey confidence in the moves you've made because teams and organizations don't handle uncertainty very well. But that doesn't mean you can't question your decisions in private. It's vital to do that. It's also critical to avoid falling prey to your own confirmation bias. We all tend to pay more attention to evidence that supports what we already think and discount data that conflicts with it. The remedy is to systematically seek out evidence that negates your hypotheses or beliefs. Throughout my career, I would push my own thinking further by listening hard to people with opinions contrary to mine or those who were bringing "inconvenient" data to a conversation. I would also ask trusted friends and colleagues what they thought about my decisions, knowing that if they saw flaws in my thinking, they wouldn't hesitate to let me know.

I wish I could say I was perfect at questioning my own beliefs, but I wasn't. Never rest on your laurels. Always challenge yourself, asking, "What if my hypotheses, assumptions, beliefs, or decisions are wrong?" If you really are right, you'll feel even more confident about it. And if you're wrong, you'll get the prodding you need to push your thinking—and your business—in a new direction.

If you set an example of rigor in your own thinking, you'll see a trickle-down effect, first among your direct reports and then among employees at lower levels. Because I demanded a lot of the teams that reported to me, those leaders became used to thinking harder and preparing more for meetings. Sometimes people need a bit of prodding in order to think more broadly or deeply.

Do you strive to understand the drawbacks of a proposed decision, asking, "What could go wrong?" Do you solicit input from every participant, even if it conflicts with your beliefs or the team's consensus? In deciding how extensively to debate an issue, do you differentiate between decisions that might have minimal consequences (thus potentially requiring less debate) and those that might produce extreme, irreversible consequences (thus requiring more debate)?

Are you as alert as you should be to evidence that conflicts with your own ideas or beliefs? What initiatives aren't working as well as you might think? Get out there and find out!

WHAT'S YOUR MEETING MINDSET?

You can take additional steps to get your people thinking harder and to shift the level of intellectual discourse among teams. Pay more attention to how you run meetings. Do you tend to dominate the conversation and dictate answers to your team? If so, you're reducing the amount or quality of thinking that is taking place. The quality of your decision-making will decline, and you'll miss a valuable opportunity to enhance your team's critical thinking capacity.

The same holds true if you reveal your own opinions on the issues before you too early—team members will come forward with ideas they think you'll like and will fail to share opinions they perceive as at odds with your own. As I like to say, it's important to be right at the end of a meeting, not at the beginning.[1] If you

1. I stumbled onto this approach when I first arrived at Honeywell. Realizing I couldn't trust my board or staff, I became a lot more careful about expressing my

embrace that mindset, you'll do a lot less talking in meetings, and focus instead on getting others to report facts and air their opinions. That of course means controlling your own ego. If you struggle in this area, remember: as a leader you get measured on the quality of your decisions and the results they produce, not on whether an idea was originally yours.[2] Be very cautious of people who come in after the meeting to tell you something they didn't think they could say in the meeting in an attempt to reverse a decision.

---◇---

Do you tend to listen to the last person with whom you've spoken, after they didn't take the opportunity to speak up during a meeting?

Do you focus on being right at the end of the meeting instead of at the beginning of the meeting?

---

opinions up front. Then I realized I was making better decisions because I was allowing for a richer discussion. I proceeded to permanently change how I ran meetings.

2. It's especially important to follow this approach when working with external advisors, bankers, or consultants of any kind. You're paying for their advice, not their endorsement. If you refrain at first from declaring your opinion and let them talk, you're more likely to get their unvarnished thoughts.

CONTROL YOUR EGO

My dad was a strong, tough guy—he had served in the US Navy in World War II, had seen a lot of action, and had been wounded. When I was a kid, I spent a lot of time working at the service station he ran. One day business was unusually slow, and we sat together on the curb waiting for something to happen. Sure enough, a car came screaming in. My dad went over and offered up his usual cheery greeting. The customer got out of the car, and for the next five minutes proceeded to berate my father for something he had done. I watched, incredulous and convinced my father would sock the man in the face. Dad was not the kind of guy to be pushed around. Instead, he became extremely apologetic, saying over and over again, "I'm sorry, I'll make it right." The customer drove off in a huff, and Dad came back to the curb. We sat there as he stared off into space—I sure wasn't going to say anything. Dejectedly, he said, "Dave, sometimes in life and in business, you have to put your pride in your back pocket."

That moment has always stuck with me. To be effective as leaders, we all have to put our egos to the side at times, no matter how tough or strong we might be.

---◇---

Think about a time you should've put your ego to the side. How could the situation have benefited from a controlled ego?

What things can you do to keep your ego controlled so you react appropriately next time you're tested?

MANAGING DIFFERENT OPINIONS

I agree with the saying, "if two people always agree, only one is thinking." When people made statements that ran counter to what I was thinking, I pushed them to develop those arguments to the fullest. When they articulated a view that conformed to my thinking, I held my tongue and didn't rush to agree with them. I developed a practice of listening all the way through and waiting three seconds to respond—it's amazing how that small change allows you to really hear what someone is saying . . . or not saying. I also registered the body language and facial expressions of others around the table, seeking valuable clues on whose opinion to solicit next.

As conversations unfolded, I did my best to draw out everyone present, including introverts who might have been struggling to participate. In so doing, I tried to remain mindful of the specific situation I was confronting as a leader and tailored my questions or comments accordingly. Many leaders tend to evoke the same persona in every meeting, but that's a mistake.

Once all the ideas were on the table, I went around and asked each participant what decision they would make if they were me. To avoid junior employees from echoing what their bosses said, I started with the most junior people and continued until I'd heard from the senior-most person. Then, and only then, did I share the decision to which I'd come. I'd explain my thinking in some detail. That way people would understand my thought process and would be better able to apply it to other decisions they might face.

To maintain the quality of our conversations, I made it clear we rewarded results, not effort. Too often individuals and teams want credit for working a hundred hours a week, irrespective of whether they actually accomplish anything. They confuse activity or effort with results, in the process distracting others from focusing on results and the actions required to achieve them. I also required people to back up their arguments with data to the extent possible.

—————◇—————

Do you challenge yourself and others to think about execution, or are you content being a strategist? Are you delegating, or abdicating?

Do you get out in the field enough to understand what's happening in operations, with your customers, and with other aspects of your business?

INCLUDE SPECIAL EXERCISES

B eyond the standard meetings I would hold, I sometimes found it necessary to lead teams through special exercises to spur their thinking around specific subjects. Even the best teams get stuck intellectually. On one occasion I had asked the purchasing team in our Aerospace unit to provide me with a long list of ideas we could adopt over time to cut costs. Months passed, and after repeated requests on my part, they were "still working on it." Having had enough, I ordered team members to cancel all their meetings for the rest of the week. The next morning, they were going to go into their conference room at 8:00 A.M. and stay there all day until they had analyzed $1.5 billion in current costs and come up with ideas for aggressively saving money in these areas. If they hadn't generated these ideas by 5:00 P.M., they'd come in the next day to continue thinking on it. It wound up taking them two days, but they came up with the ideas. They just needed a little friendly encouragement from me.

When teams were struggling to envision a potentially different future, I would use a different technique, what I refer to as my "White Sheet of Paper" exercise. The name says it all: I asked teams to take a step back and reimagine their businesses from scratch. Often when teams have trouble creatively it's because their thinking is overly constricted by reality as they know it and they can only think of ideas that derive from the existing reality. I'd ask them to take a day and pretend they could build their business, process, or product from scratch. What would it look like? How would they design it? Usually suspending reality broke the logjam and allowed people to think of a future that was very different from the present.

Once teams specify both their present position and desired destination, it becomes much easier to lay out the logical steps, the resources the team will need, and a realistic timeline for getting there.

———◇———

Can you spot opportunities to reanchor your people using the White Sheet of Paper exercise?

Where might you profitably accelerate progress by "locking people in the room" and requiring that they produce a solution?

INSTILL AN INTELLECTUAL MINDSET

In organizations beset by short-termism, leaders often fail to invest sufficiently in Growth Initiatives, process initiatives, and other growth programs. Spending in those areas detracts from the quarterly numbers, and the returns don't show up until many quarters, or even years, later.

The quality of thought in a team or organization matters. If you want a business that performs both today *and* tomorrow, you need to take apart your business and put it back together again so that it works more efficiently and effectively. That means instilling an intellectual mindset, spurring your people to think harder about every business decision they face. Set the standard for intellectual engagement. Demand that your people pursue two seemingly conflicting things at the same time.

Make it your mission to understand the nuances of your

businesses so that you can shape and guide your teams' intellectual inquiry. Allocate your time thoughtfully; don't become a victim of your calendar. Carve out time to read, research, and *think*. Turn your meetings into vigorous, instructive debates. As you'll find, performing today *and* tomorrow is hard, but it's not impossible. You just need to put your mind to it. You need the right *mindset*.

————————◇————————

What are two to three ways you can instill an intellectual mindset within your team?

Once a week, carve out time to read, research, and think. Put your mind to instilling an intellectual mindset for yourself. Block off time on your calendar right now.

OVERCOMING SHORT-TERMISM

To overcome an entrenched short-termism, it's not enough to inculcate a mindset of intellectual inquiry and honesty into the organization. You also must embed this mindset and a commitment to both short- and long-term goals deep into strategic planning. Unless leaders at every level and in every part of the business know they must take planning seriously as an intellectual exercise, and unless they are oriented toward planting seeds for the future even as they reap today's harvests, they'll give themselves a pass. They'll sign on to unrealistic long-term goals that make them look good to their superiors, then take ill-advised shortcuts to make short-term numbers.

It's up to leaders at every level to define what a proper strategy looks like, and to give the organization the processes, funding, and analytic tools it needs to deliver results. This isn't easy or glamorous work, but it must be done if you want your business to perform well years into the future while pleasing investors today.

———————◇———————

What kind of short-term, "make the quarter" activities do you see in your organization? Are they hurting long-term effectiveness?

MAKE STRATEGY PART
OF DAILY WORK

E very leader should take steps to make the planning process more regular and substantive. By setting aside growth and operations days for myself, I created time in my schedule as well as in that of my staff to hold follow-up consultations and requested reports. Our follow-up consultations required staff to gather and analyze data regularly throughout the year. Strategy shouldn't be a one-time, annual event that occurs during an annual review, assessment, or at the end of a fiscal year.

You can plan for today and tomorrow at any level—whether you lead a business unit, a department, or a small team. If you run the payroll department at a company, ask yourself each year how you could handle an increasing volume of work while keeping fixed costs steady. How can you redesign your processes and systems so that you reduce errors, use fewer people, and are generally more effective? Generate some ideas, and then develop a strategic plan to implement them, as well as an operating budget. Find a way to reduce costs elsewhere within your organization to self-fund at least a portion of your ideas. Bring your ideas to your bosses and sell them, describing how you'll start slow, make sustainable progress, and see sizable performance gains over time.

As I like to say, modifying a famous statement of Thomas Edison's, "Business is 1 percent strategy and 99 percent execution." Take the time you need up front to get the strategy right so that you can then get the execution right. In particular, when staff present summaries for their strategies, have them highlight what has changed in comparison with previous strategies. Organizations that shift their strategy every couple of years become directionless and ineffectual. By taking extra time to ensure that your strategy makes sense and spending just a bit of time daily validating it, your organization can spend 99 percent of its time executing instead of failing.

———◇———

How might you encourage people to reflect upon next year's results at the beginning of this year rather than at the end?

LEGACY ISSUES

Honeywell should have been seen not merely as an environmentally friendly company but as a world leader in sustainability, but many members of the public didn't like us. After all, the products and services we sold (and still sell) helped the world reduce emissions, generate green energy, defend the country, and protect the ozone layer. Because of our handling of legacy issues, however, our brand image was terrible. At around the time when I became CEO, we were facing several criminal and near-criminal investigations. In 2003, the District Court of New Jersey rendered a decision sharply criticizing our handling of environmental issues and ordered us to conduct a massive cleanup at a site in Jersey City.

In other communities around the country, environmental and asbestos lawsuits yielded vast amounts of bad press for us. A 2003 op-ed in the local Syracuse, New York, newspaper warned of "lakeside toxic tombs" at Honeywell-owned sites, while a 2004 article in the *Arizona Republic* carried the headline "Honeywell Sued on Toxic

Fuel."[5] In the latter article, the state's attorney general was quoted as saying that "Honeywell seemed to think they could tell the regulators anything they wanted with impunity and not be bound by the truth." Not terribly flattering. And as you can imagine, such stories didn't win us plaudits from employees either.

You might wonder whether previous generations of leaders had experienced pangs of conscience about failing to deal with legacy issues like pollution or asbestos. If they did, I didn't hear about it. Maybe someday these issues would be permanently resolved, but that wasn't our problem. We needed to focus on performing *now*.

If you're running a team or organization with legacy issues, don't think like this. Younger generations of employees and consumers expect transparency from companies, and they have less tolerance than ever for leaders and organizations that shirk their social responsibility. Companies that step up to repair the harm they've caused and prevent new harm from occurring attract top talent. It's probably going to be cheaper for your organization to resolve your legacy issues now than it will be a decade from now, when the harm will have mounted even more. But if none of this convinces you to take action, think about *your* legacy. What kind of leader do you want to be? Do you want to be known as the leader who passed the buck and feigned ignorance? Or do you want to be known as the one who had the courage to do what others wouldn't, even if it bit into short-term results?

When you make big decisions, are you thinking about minimizing risks to your business years, even decades, down the road? Are you ignoring any potential time bombs?

Is your business really living up to the lofty ideals enshrined in your mission or vision statements? Are employees or others noting the contradictions?

ENLIST EMPLOYEES TO IMPROVE PROCESSES

As I knew from my days as an hourly factory worker, the majority of workers want to do a great job and use their minds to improve weak or wasteful processes. But in traditional manufacturing environments, they lack formal processes and procedures for doing so. I had operated a machine that punched out little pieces of metal. What were these pieces for? Where did they go after they left my station? Damned if I knew. Managers expected me to do my job, but I didn't receive much instruction, nor did I get a sense of the broader picture of my plant. Managers didn't expect me to actually *think* about what I was doing, and they didn't give me a voice in improving my job or the plant's overall operations.

Later when I became the CEO of Honeywell, the strategy of enlisting employees' help in improving processes occurred to me. I thought immediately of the Toyota Production System (TPS), the automaker's legendary system for improving processes at its plants to reduce waste and improve efficiency and effectiveness.[6] When issues arose, employees could immediately bring them to managers' attention and be assured that managers would take those issues seriously and work to resolve them. Workers had a chance to participate in *kaizen* events that helped them understand the larger processes to which their jobs contributed and that allowed them to provide input as to how those processes might be run differently or better. TPS also emphasized making sure that plants were clean and orderly, and that work was standardized to the extent possible.

I wondered if we might connect with Toyota to see if we could learn more about TPS and incorporate elements of it into a new operating system for Honeywell. Later that year, a group of our high-level leaders in manufacturing, purchasing, and logistics went to Toyota's training facility. What these leaders saw impressed them. The plant was clean and clearly marked, with teams tracking performance on work boards and via quality checks within production lines. Most importantly, the people were "engaged in the process. It wasn't all top-down . . . These were fully engaged employees, fully engaged management." Because the work was standardized, people "knew what they were supposed to do, and they took ownership."[7]

Based on my experience, I would recommend implementing changes in phases. This will give you the opportunity to determine what works and why. Most people hate to work with inefficient, ineffective processes—they want to go home each night to their families and proudly talk about what they have accomplished. By giving employees the chance to engage mentally with their work and to be part of a team that worked *better* together, both retention and morale will improve.

—————◇—————

Do you have a system in place for constantly improving processes? How well does it work? Do you empower frontline workers to improve how work gets done?

GO DEEP ON PROCESS

If you wish to improve operations in your organization, proceed deliberately. Focus on transforming the culture so process change becomes permanent. It's so important to do process improvement right. If you don't, you don't merely waste resources and stagnate as an organization—you stand a strong chance of moving backward. Bad process improvement is devastating. As people discover they haven't made progress, they become even more dispirited and unmotivated than they had been. Customers suffer, forced to navigate processes that have become even more ineffective. As some of these customers leave, business results slide. Meanwhile, companies find that they need to re-implement process change again after a few years because it didn't stick the first time. Such failures cost money and reinforce the notion that process change is merely a passing fancy among management.

Rather than implementing your initiative the way organizations commonly do, first immerse yourself in the details to discover what works for *your* organization. As tempting as it might be to rush, test and refine how you're rolling out major operational changes, and build a track record of success that can get others in your organization excited about the change. Also, put resources behind it. As the old saying goes, if you make a change initiative everyone's part-time job, you get part-time results. We wanted full-time results, so we put the necessary people and money behind it . . . full time.

With a strong implementation plan in place, keep a close eye on how your process improvement initiative is progressing. Never take change for granted. Facilities have no problem generating nice-sounding stories about the changes they're making. But what do the numbers say? Is the change as profound as plant leaders think? And is it persisting? Entropy is the rule in organizations, as it is in the physical universe. Over time, all organized systems evolve toward chaos. Unless you pursue change relentlessly, your efforts will eventually wither away.

———◇———

Have you structured your process improvement initiative in such a way to sustain improvement over time? Are you personally verifying that it is working?

Is your team or organization adept at constantly evolving, or do you cling too closely to the operational status quo?

REVOLUTIONARY CHANGE ISN'T THE WAY TO MOVE

Revolutionary change sounds good, but it's not the optimal route to strong short- and long-term performance. If you go with revolutionary change, you're taking a huge risk, because you can never be exactly sure what the future holds. Revolutions can move in unintended directions. An organization that is adept at constantly evolving usually won't need to take enormous risks to bring about revolutionary change, because it'll have been changing all along. Think of it this way: If various dimensions of your market are changing, say, 4 percent a year, that might not sound like a lot. However, if you don't change with it, or better yet, stay slightly ahead of the change, then these changes will compound year after year. A decade down the line, you'll be looking at an enormous gap between where you are and where your market is. Then revolutionary change, and all the risk and disruption it entails, really will be necessary just to catch up. Sometimes a revolution is required depending on the state of your business or organization, but it's far better to keep pace with change as it occurs or to stay ahead of it, and to develop an organization that is committed to and capable of constant, incremental evolution.

When I took over at Honeywell, some people thought the company might well go extinct before too long. We managed to grow and flourish because we challenged ourselves through process change and cultural transformation to constantly improve what we did, and to get better at improving over time. Enhancing our processes incrementally and sustainably became part of our culture at Honeywell, informing how we ran everything about the company. If you work at it, you can make it part of your culture too.

———◇———

Before today, what was your opinion on revolutionary change? Have you experienced an instance when revolutionary change severely impacted a business? What did you learn?

CREATING CULTURE

As obvious as it sounds, you should start your culture-building efforts by defining the culture you want. During my second month at Honeywell, I created the five key strategic initiatives I wanted the company to focus on and a list of twelve behaviors I wanted to define our culture.

The Five Initiatives

1. Growth (via customer service, globalization, and technology)
2. Productivity (goes hand-in-hand with growth)
3. Cash (improve working capital and have high-quality earnings)
4. People (keep the best talent, organized the right way and motivated)

5. Enablers (including Six Sigma, Honeywell Operating System, and Functional Transformation)

The Twelve Behaviors

1. Focus on customers and growth (serve customers well and aggressively pursue growth).
2. Lead impactfully (think like a leader and serve as a role model).
3. Get results (consistently meet any commitments that you make).
4. Make people better (encourage excellence in peers, subordinates, and/or managers).
5. Champion change (drive continuous improvement in our operations).
6. Foster teamwork and diversity (define *success* in terms of the entire team).
7. Adopt a global mindset (view the business from all relevant perspectives, and see the world in terms of integrated value chains).
8. Take risks intelligently (recognize that we must take greater but smarter risks to generate better returns).
9. Be self-aware (recognize your behavior and how it affects those around you).

10. Communicate effectively (provide information to others in a timely, concise, and thoughtful way).
11. Think in an integrative fashion (make more holistic decisions beyond your own bailiwick by applying intuition, experience, and judgment to the available data).
12. Develop technical or functional excellence (be capable and effective in your particular area of expertise).

As a team we fleshed out the details. We made it clear that everyone on the team had a chance to contribute and that their opinions mattered.

Do you truly have a high-performing culture? Do employees, managers, and leaders really believe in it, or do they just pay lip service? Are they committed to the organization, or does unmitigated self-interest reign? Is your culture really driving the performance you want?

If you have a long-established culture, is it still working for you? Are certain behaviors or attitudes missing in your definition?

SPREAD THE CULTURE—AND SPREAD IT SOME MORE

You can never organize perfectly to ensure that all potential interactions happen across functions, product lines, processes, geographies, and so on. But you can work hard to ensure that as many people as possible get to know one another. Distrust kills cooperation, and it prevails when people are sequestered from one another. The more trust you build and the more widespread your desired culture becomes, the greater the chances that the thousands of decisions people make every day will break the way you'd like them to.

As a leader, you should make culture your personal mission. As important as it is to enmesh your desired culture into processes and structures, you also have to communicate it personally. Many leaders know this, but they don't always work as intensely as they should to highlight the culture for employees and managers. Acculturation doesn't occur because people rationally imbibe information that's thrown at them. They do it because they see principles or ideas in action. Leaders should always be mindful of their behavior and whether it accorded within their own Twelve Behaviors.

How much time do you personally spend on culture-building activities? Are you driving it home on a daily basis—in meetings, in casual conversations, in your decision-making, and at formal events? Has your own commitment to culture lagged over time? Do you take every opportunity, even if it seems like a waste of time, to reinforce your needed culture?

DON'T LET YOUR
CULTURE LIMIT YOU

I n driving for cultural change, it's a mistake to become overly constrained by your desired culture as you've defined it. Are there any other related behaviors, values, or principles that support high performance than the ones you've formally adopted? If so, don't hesitate to push these as well.

Timeliness wasn't one of our Twelve Behaviors, but an organization in which meetings start late and teams miss deadlines probably isn't going to be successful. In other organizations I've worked in, late meetings tended to have a ripple effect across the organizations, preventing other meetings from taking place as planned and causing all kinds of operational chaos. People were constantly rescheduling everything—a huge waste of time and energy. Leaders would waste their time showing up at meetings in which other relevant actors weren't present. If nothing else, time-liness is a basic sign of respect, a recognition that other people's time is as important as yours.

Another concept that wasn't reflected in the Twelve Behaviors but that we pushed extraordinarily hard was integrity. To perform well, you need to build trusting relationships with customers, investors, suppliers, employees, governments, and the communities in which you operate—really, with whomever you deal with. That means adopting metrics that accurately measure the reality of your performance and adopting more transparency in your accounting practices. It also means keeping promises you make to local communities to clean up. Critically, it also means complying with the applicable laws in all the countries in which you operate.

———◇———

If you have been doggedly building your culture, are there some additional supportive values or concepts that you might also emphasize for your workforce?

HIRING

When making hiring decisions or promoting employees, make talent decisions in ways that support the culture without acting too aggressively. In organizations, too much change too quickly can leave people reeling. Although I did wind up changing many of our top leaders in an effort to build a high-performance culture, I tried to balance the need for change with the need for stability. You should do the same. Push change as fast as possible, but not so fast that the changes fail to take root.

It's also important to mobilize hiring as a means of building the culture you want. With a robust performance culture in place, you stand a much greater chance that people will make decisions the way you wish they would. Culture doesn't merely yield results but helps sustain them.

———◇———

How strong are your underlying "people processes"? Do any of them need revamping in order to better deliver the culture?

Are you paying too much attention to external candidates when filling key posts?

CREATE A SUCCESSION PLAN

M ost companies have succession plans for their leadership ranks, but it devolves into a rote exercise, and the organization lacks a clear sense of who will fill key roles in case of departure. It's another instance of what I call "compliance with words rather than compliance with intent." As a leader, my team and I put deep thought into our succession planning. As a result, we never required more than a couple of days to name a successor when high-level executives departed. That helped us avoid the period of ambiguity that departures commonly trigger, as well as the resulting disruption.

It's critically important to make leadership transitions rapid and seamless. In the month or two (or longer) it might take to fill a key role, and then the month or longer it takes for a new leader to get settled, organizations typically stagnate. Nobody works all that hard, so short-term goals suffer and long-term initiatives that had been steaming ahead lose momentum. Although leaders often regard such stagnation as inevitable, a fact of life inside organizations, it really isn't. To avoid the hit to performance, prepare far in advance so that you don't miss a beat when someone leaves.

If you want to perform well over both the short and long term, pay close attention to executive leadership in general. As much as you might invest in areas like culture and process transformation, you'll only make progress if you have talented senior leaders who are both committed to the company's strategies and capable of executing on them. Having the right *number* of those leaders matters too. You should keep fixed costs constant while increasing sales. Just as you're pushing for more efficiency throughout the organization via process change, you can also keep your organization increasingly slender and nimble as you grow by maintaining a leadership corps that is relatively small and stable but that punches far above its weight. Enhance the quality of leaders rather than their sheer quantity, and you'll increase your organization's ability to adapt, compete, and perform over *every* time frame.

---◇---

Do you perform succession planning with enough rigor and vigor? Is your organization frequently unsettled by departing leaders? If your best people left tomorrow, how long would it take you to lock in replacements?

MAKE PERFORMANCE
REVIEWS MEANINGFUL

Bosses should do the actual work of appraising how well their employees are doing. Leaders shouldn't use the busyness crutch as an excuse not to write up thoughtful performance reviews every year.

Having the best people makes a difference, so devoting time to writing performance reviews is a good investment of a boss's time. Completed appraisals will ensure that people are supporting the company's culture and including behavior requirements into their day-to-day.

I've found that timing appraisals in coordination with salary decisions is an effective process. Our tighter appraisal process required more effort on managers' part, but it certainly helps to boost performance at the top of the organization, while also yielding a more accurate picture of leadership quality at any given time.

———◇———

Do you and your business take performance reviews seriously? Does your business time these reviews to align with salary actions?

HOLD PEOPLE ACCOUNTABLE & BEWARE OF UPWARD DELEGATION

About twenty years ago, *Harvard Business Review* published a great article about the phenomenon of upward delegation called "Who's Got the Monkey?"[8] Subpar performers love to evade or at least share responsibility for tasks by consulting with their superiors, in the guise of asking for advice. This can take a couple of different forms. In some cases, they'll send you a seemingly innocuous email explaining a problem, or raise this problem in a meeting, asking, "What do you want to do?" In these situations, you must always put the onus back on them to come up with a solution. Ask them to identify various options and explain the logic behind each, and request that they make a recommendation. If you don't do this, they'll think you now bear responsibility for the decision.

Alternately, some reports will ask for your opinion on the thought process they went through in arriving at a decision. This might well be their attempt to get you to co-own the decision, even though you likely don't know all of the relevant information as well as they do. When it comes time for a performance review, they'll then point to this conversation to claim co-ownership to evade responsibility for poor performance. Don't fall for this trick. In such situations, I would offer my opinion, but also put the responsibility squarely back on my reports' shoulders, saying something like, "That sounds right, but just to be clear, the decision is on you, not on me. You are the person on the ground so you have to sort it out, and you're also responsible for the results."

———◇———

Are you careful not to let subordinates delegate upward in either emails or in-person conversations?

DON'T HOLD ON TO
POOR PERFORMERS

Performance reviews will do little to improve the quality of your team if you don't address subpar performance when you encounter it. I've witnessed organizations being too soft with underperformers, allowing ineffective or bad employees to continue in their posts. The reasons varied: bosses cringed at having difficult conversations, they felt bad for the ineffective employees, and they believed certain leaders were too valuable to let go despite their bad behavior. The reality is, nobody is indispensable. I myself let go of a couple of key employees and leaders who were delivering their numbers yet failing to support our cultural values. As we told senior executives, if they were afraid or reluctant to let ineffective employees go—if they wanted to give them another chance—they needed to consider the lives and careers of the thousands of people working alongside, as well as the duty we collectively owed to shareholders and customers to perform well.

As a rule, the negative effects of poor performers spread far and wide, because others perceive that the threshold of what an organization will tolerate is lower than they thought. By removing poor performers, you and your team remind everyone that your standards are high—a lesson I learned when I was an hourly employee. My coworkers and I all knew who the weakest performer in our group was. When that person was let go, we scrambled to make sure we weren't now the weakest!

Underperforming leaders (and lower-level managers and employees as well) should take responsibility for fixing their own performance. If they don't change within a fairly quick time period, they should face the consequences. That might sound cold and uncompromising, but it really isn't—it's honoring and supporting the vast majority of people who *are* working hard and performing.

———◇———

Do you take a hard line with underperformers? Do you amply reward your top performers?

PROVIDE FEEDBACK IN A WAY RECIPIENTS CAN INTERNALIZE

Too many leaders expect their people to adapt to their particular leadership style. If you want the best performance, look beyond your style and provide feedback tailored to the individual. With some employees, you have to be loud to get their attention. With others, all you need to say is, "You are capable of better work than this." Being loud at the latter isn't going to help. And treating the former too politely may elicit a grunt but no discernible behavior changes. Know your people well, and adapt your feedback accordingly.

Speaking of feedback, experts often advise that leaders should "criticize privately and praise publicly." Criticizing privately might be appropriate in certain sensitive cases, but in general both criticism and praise should be public. Your people have to understand that certain behaviors or performance are unacceptable. Otherwise they'll wonder why the organization allows it. When leaders share both criticism and praise publicly, team members learn about the high-performance culture you're striving to create.

---◇---

How can you tailor feedback to your individual employees? Think about the best way to get each individual's attention so they can internalize your feedback.

Do people in a meeting know when you're unhappy about something and why?

PAY WELL

I've always believed that money alone doesn't suffice to motivate talented people, because the majority of us also want fulfilling, meaningful work. To get the best people, you must pay them extremely well for what they do *and* give them jobs and a workplace environment they love.

I've encountered agencies that prefer a more formulaic approach when calculating compensation. Some "experts" believe the best way to determine compensation is to benchmark it directly to a company's stock market performance in a given year. If the stock is the 75th percentile as compared with its peers, then compensation for leaders should be below the 75th percentile. That's silly.

First, the stock market isn't a good short-term proxy for performance. Second, you can't chart performance on a proportional scale. A football player who runs the forty-yard-dash in 4.3 seconds is only 2 percent faster than one who runs it in 4.4 seconds—maybe in the 100th percentile versus the 98th. But that one-tenth of a second and two percentile points make all the difference between winning or losing the Super Bowl, between catching the ball or being intercepted. Small differences in performance can have a big impact, in business as well as sports, and we need to acknowledge that in how we compensate leaders.

If a compensation plan pays out well, directors and compensation consultants sometimes assume the plan wasn't rigorous enough. A well-constructed plan, they suggest, would pay out exactly 100 percent of projected compensation; otherwise, the original goals were obviously too easy to meet. How absurd! It's true the original goals might have been too easy, but perhaps the higher payouts reflected exceptional performance relative to a leader's peers. If your compensation plan is always paying out 100 percent of compensation, you risk disappointing your exceptional leaders, who feel they've been outperforming but are not being paid for it. If the performance is there, pay for it! Fairness requires nothing less.

---◇---

Are you paying your best leaders enough?

Are you creating the conditions required for them to succeed?

HIRE DELIBERATELY & FIND THE TOM BRADY WITHIN

As important as retention is, you must also hire the right people to begin with—a task that requires considerable thought, effort, and commitment. So often busy leaders compromise on the selection process. When a key job opens up and the organization is scrambling, they throw up their hands and say, "Hiring somebody is better than nobody." That might seem true in the short term, but only because you feel better having someone in the position. In reality, the wrong somebody causes a great deal of pain. It's far better to leave a job open for a few months to get the very best person and deal with the disruption that causes, than to settle for mediocrity.

So often organizations overlook the talent right in front of them, stereotyping them because of their credentials or past positions. When quarterback Tom Brady joined the New England Patriots football team, nobody knew who he was. During his first season with the team, he sat on the bench as the star quarterback led the team to a losing record. Then the star quarterback got injured, and the team turned to this nobody named Brady. The Patriots began to win, and they wound up battling their way to the organization's first-ever Super Bowl victory. Brady went on to lead the team to eight more Super Bowls, winning five of them, for six total, and emerged as one of the greatest quarterbacks in football history. Here was a Hall of Fame player sitting on the bench for a year, his superior talent unrecognized—and this in a business that is exceedingly rigorous in how it evaluates talent.

In business, it's easy to write off people in your organization for big jobs because they don't have experience, or because they never got an MBA, or because they got an MBA from a second-tier state school, or because they've performed well in a particular job and you have them unfairly stereotyped. As I like to say, in my experience, experience is overrated. Just a little bit of experience combined with a lot of raw talent is worth far more.

In deciding whom to hire at Honeywell, we focused on building teams that would work well together, adding people with certain personal qualities that would balance out or complement those of our existing staff. If a given team had a decisive leader, we would seek to put in place people around him or her who were more deliberate by nature, and vice versa.

When it comes to understanding the personality types of team members, we used the Myers-Briggs test, which in my view is the best tool in the world.

———◇———

Do you actively seek out the Tom Bradys already in your organization?

Do you personally interview candidates for important positions?

SMART ISN'T ENOUGH

M any companies look to hire smart people when filling leadership roles. And yet, being a good leader takes more than just intelligence. Smart leaders get beaten every day by others who have better judgment, less ego, and more common sense; who pay more attention to execution and detail; who possess better interpersonal skills; and who can recover from setbacks better, think more independently, and work harder.

Learn how to use all these skills as you lead people and run meetings to arrive at good decisions. And just as importantly, hire people who have those capabilities in addition to being smart. Oh, and be sure to pick people who have something to prove to the world. As the adage goes, it's easier to take a bit of wind out of someone's sails than to put wind into their sails to begin with.

———————◇———————

Have you been managed by someone who thought they were the smartest person in the company? If yes, how are you doing things differently? How has that leadership changed your own leadership views?

ALWAYS STRIVE TO PLEASE YOUR CUSTOMERS

I first became attuned to the importance of pleasing customers at the age of twelve while working in my dad's garage. I cleaned windshields, kept the bathroom tidy, and helped put the tools in the garage bays back in their place after cleaning them. When I asked Dad why I was doing all the unpleasant jobs, he told me I had to start at the bottom to understand everything. And he also told me washing windshields was quite important work. People could buy their gas anywhere, so we needed to give them a good reason to come to our shop. A nice, clean windshield was a way for us to set ourselves apart in customers' eyes.

Likewise, when customers went to the restroom and found it clean, they felt better about getting their car serviced with us—it was a visual reminder that we took pride in what we did. Dad also insisted we treat customers with courtesy and respect. "Remember," he used to say, "the higher up the flagpole you climb, the more people can see your ass." Colorful, but I got the message. Be nice to everyone—especially customers.

---◇---

Are your customers as happy as everyone says they are? How do you know? Have you gotten out there recently to ask them for their candid feedback? How good are your customer-related metrics?

Is your culture as customer focused as it could be?

METRICS ARE TRICKIER
THAN THEY SEEM

O ur initial difficulties with customer experience at Honeywell illustrated an important concept about measurement. Some people say that "what gets measured gets done." Which is not necessarily true. We discussed this in an earlier entry. If you measure something, the metric will improve because people learn to adjust and redefine, "playing" to the metric. As I like to say, if you measure something, the metric will get better. If you announce you want 50 percent of sales to come from products introduced over the previous three years, you'll find people redefining new products or coming out with new model numbers for the same old products with slight modifications, and bingo—you're at 50 percent with no substantive change. In other words, metrics often foster compliance with words rather than with intent. The only fix is to set clear definitions up front and implement some kind of audit process.

The customer experience should be front and center, so it is framed as an essential part of the high-performance culture you're building. Businesses that thrive cannot afford to blame someone else for their internal problems. When problems arise, leaders must identify the root causes of issues and change their processes to fix them. The effort will make a difference.

Pay attention to your metrics in retrospect to your customer experience. If your metrics improve but you receive more customer service complaints, there is a problem. This is why metrics are trickier than they seem. While paying attention to the measurement product sales, you must also pay attention to the metric of customer satisfaction.

———◇———

Think of one way you can improve your customer experience. What effort will it require from you and your team?

Are there operational metrics that may be providing rosier views than reality? How can you make all metrics used to run your business robust and reliable indicators of real performance?

PAY ATTENTION TO
THE END USER

One way we improved R&D was by getting our people focused on delivering a better user experience. During the late 1990s, I had a Honeywell thermostat in my home that was blasting the air-conditioning during the summer, to the point where it was too cold. When I tried to adjust the thermostat, I couldn't figure out how to do it. I looked at the instructions printed on the panel and found it confusing, not to mention that the print was minuscule. When I consulted the owner's manual, I couldn't for the life of me figure out how to dial up the temperature setting. Finally, I gave up and put on a sweater.

When I became CEO, we discussed improving the user experience during one of our early strategic planning reviews, but with so many other priorities demanding attention, user experience faded to the background. Then, almost a decade later, while teaching a leadership class at West Point, the U.S. Military Academy (an incredible honor for this small-town boy), I heard a professor talk about how good the school was in teaching "human factors," or the discipline devoted to making everyday objects better suited ergonomically to human users. Here, I thought, was an area that we at Honeywell hadn't yet focused on—and one that represented a potentially important pathway to sales growth. Companies like Apple were great at anticipating important, often unspoken customer needs and incorporating them into product design. If we were to maximize our sales, we couldn't just have more new products rolled out more quickly. We needed *better* new products that were easier to use, install, and maintain, which in turn meant we had to understand customer needs more deeply. We had to improve the *experience* of the user, installer, and maintainer.

There is an important lesson: even if you and your team develop good ideas and initiatives to improve, leaders must still push relentlessly for people to go beyond daily operations and take the initiative seriously. In order to achieve growth in your business, you must be willing to think critically about how your organization can create new products and services and how you might do it more swiftly and better.

———◇———

How much attention do your product development people pay to the actual experience of using your product or service? Are you inside the heads of customers as fully as you might be to understand their unspoken needs?

PICK YOUR GROWTH PRIORITIES

I n every business there are several avenues to growth. Companies can't pursue them all with the same level of intensity at any given time. It's important to prioritize. As you start to invest in growth initiatives, take stock of your company and its strengths and weaknesses, identifying your greatest growth opportunities. Perhaps your flow of new products is already great and so is your customer service, but you don't have much of a business in a particular country you think could be big for you. Start there, and as I've suggested, make a targeted effort. Of course, that requires patience. To return to one of my favorite metaphors, you can till the soil and plant seeds, but then you have to water the plants and care for them over a full season and sometimes several seasons as they grow—no shortcuts.

You can't delegate away responsibility for growth and expect to see results. The prospect of growth excites people inside organizations, but as you proceed, the changes required will arouse resistance or fall prey to inertia amid the press of daily operations.

Don't forget about the challenges you'll encounter along the way. Challenges will pop up when we least expect it. Lastly, make sure the actions people are taking in support of these initiatives really are yielding results. You don't pursue something for its own sake. You do it to drive sales. And yet it's easy for people in the trenches to conflate all the hard work they might be doing with actual results. If the initiative is going so well, what does the sales increase look like? Never stop posing such questions to your people.

———◇———

If you're just beginning to focus on growth, what are your company's existing strengths and opportunities? Where might you get the most bang for your long-term growth investments? How do you allocate sufficient money and people to those initiatives?

KEEP SCANNING THE HORIZON

Don't limit yourself. Stay alert for new growth areas. Midway into my tenure at Honeywell, we concluded that a digital revolution would sweep through the industrial economy in coming decades, and that we stood to gain immensely if we could get way ahead of it. In addition to expanding our software engineering in high-growth regions and bringing our engineers across the world to level 5 status, we started to work on new digital business models—like enabling and reselling Wi-Fi time on aircraft, and our Sentience platform for developing new software products. Now called Honeywell Forge, the platform is a cloud-based, IoT platform and product development framework within Honeywell for building scalable software. Standardizing the process allows developers to create new software products more expeditiously and consistently than they used to. Honeywell Forge focuses on three key areas for customers: providing end-to-end enterprise performance management for asset reliability; process excellence; and worker safety, competency, and productivity.

We also changed our recruiting practices to improve our digital talent pool. Formerly, we had sought out digital talent from the best, name-brand colleges and universities. Now we focused on attracting members of a small subset of elite programmers who were capable of producing ten times the output of the typical programmer. To attract these premier programmers, or "multipliers" as we called them, we began evaluating potential hires on specific skills related to programming, collaboration, and teamwork, observing their actual behavior rather than just relying on their academic record. We took a similar approach to hiring data scientists as well. Our efforts in this area helped us significantly up our game as we developed software as a business and incorporated it into more of our existing products.

———◇———

What opportunities are on the horizon for your industry and business? What is the next thing that will revolutionize your business? What steps can you take to get ahead and be part of new growth?

M&A: STEP ONE
BUILD A ROBUST PIPELINE
(IDENTIFICATION)

O ver the next four days, we're going to dive into the M&A process. Even if your company isn't big enough (now) to think about merging and acquisitions, this dealmaking and discipline process is essential knowledge for any leader.

Step one of the M&A process is to build a robust pipeline (identification). To land winning deals, you first have to find them. You should begin with putting strategy first, mobilizing your business units to think hard about their strategic growth goals, aggressively scour the market, and maintain a broad pipeline of desirable targets for acquisition. By "desirable," I am referring to businesses that occupy great positions—that have good market share or are on a path to getting there via future acquisitions in good, high-growth, profitable industries.

Since leaders are immersed in strategy every day, they can naturally make an ongoing investigation of acquisition opportunities part of their conversations.

To Build a Robust Pipeline . . .

- Don't wait for bankers to knock on your door with potential deals. Instead, scour the market proactively.
- Seek out businesses that have great positions in good, high-growth industries.
- Look for bolt-on acquisitions as well as companies in good industries adjacent to yours.
- Recognize that not all perceived adjacencies are the same. If the adjacency is too far removed from your existing business, you will lose your shirt.
- Make identifying targets a day-to-day priority.
- Be patient. Nurture long-term relationships with potential acquisitions.

---◇---

How well do you identify potential acquisitions? Are you and your teams constantly building a pipeline of potential companies to acquire? Do you vet these opportunities strategically?

M&A: STEP TWO
KILL BAD DEALS
(DUE DILIGENCE)

T he second step of the M&A process is making sure the potential acquisition is everything the seller says it is. When you really dig into a company and its books, do you still want to acquire it, and if so, at what price? Do you want to attach any special conditions to the deal, detailing scenarios in which you'd walk away if outstanding issues aren't addressed?

For instance, our legal team might conclude that a company we were thinking of acquiring faced potential lawsuits. Analyzing the situation, our team would identify the extent of the risk we faced, whether we could insure against it or secure indemnification, and whether we should walk away from the deal if we couldn't mitigate our risk. Our general counsel would make the call on whether the deal made sense or not.

Additionally, we changed our compensation structure, no longer paying bonuses to leaders involved in securing particular acquisitions. Such bonuses incentivize people to make deals, regardless of whether they are good or bad. We wanted people to make *good* deals and kill the bad ones.

To Kill Bad Deals . . .

- Standardize how you perform due diligence.
- Have your functional experts advise you on any potential issues.
- Don't incentivize people for getting deals done, as over time that might lead them to push through potentially questionable deals.

Do you have a clear process mapped out for performing due diligence? How receptive are you when recognizing or addressing problems with deals as they arise?

M&A: STEP THREE
NEVER OVERPAY (VALUATION)

The third step of the M&A process is creating your own model for valuing companies you're acquiring instead of relying on the valuations that investment bankers bring to you. If Honeywell bought a company and four years later the deal didn't work out the way we'd anticipated, we couldn't just tell our investors that the bankers' valuation model had been no good. We needed to create our own model, and then we needed to believe in what our model said and we had to be able to deliver on it. That meant getting in there and actually performing the valuation work ourselves.

As the leader, it should be your job to exercise final oversight over deals that have made it through the process, truly exploring the potential downsides of a deal to determine if it is worth proceeding at the price negotiated. By the time your teams have done their work and the deal is ready for your approval, the teams believe in the deal and should be quite understandably focused on the upside. While that upside might well be the most likely outcome, it is vital that you push one more time to consider what could go wrong, just to be certain everyone has considered all possible scenarios.

To Never Overpay . . .

- Develop a standardized valuation model of your own.
- Use your own estimates of sales and margins.
- Factor in anticipated cost savings, but not sales synergies.
- Value acquisitions conservatively and walk away if the deal becomes too rich.
- Don't let the dealmakers negotiate the terms.
- Exercise final oversight, exploring the downsides and scuttling the deal if you risk overpaying.
- Maintain a great pipeline of potential deals so that no single deal seems like a must-have.

———◇———

Have you overpaid in the past? Why or why not? Do you accept the numbers that acquired companies or bankers give you, or do you perform your own valuations of possible acquisitions?

M&A: STEP FOUR
GREAT TRACK RECORD
(INTEGRATION)

The fourth and final step of the M&A process is obtaining attractive cost synergies; you need to integrate acquired companies well with your existing company. To tighten up how Honeywell performed integrations, we required that each business in Honeywell that was acquiring another business had an approved integration plan in place before the deal closed. This plan had to specify the metrics we were aiming for year after year (including cost synergies, sales synergies, and so on), with the first year broken down into quarterly goals. The plan also had to cover management changes we anticipated making, changes to pay and benefits, changes to the business's functional systems, and other big moves we planned to make.

To Bring Acquisitions into the Fold . . .

- Put integration plans in place before the deal closes, covering management, metrics, and other relevant topics.
- Personally review and approve the plan.
- Tighten up the executional details.
- Put dedicated, full-time integration teams in place, and assemble these teams early.
- Make changes and communicate them immediately to shape the mindset.
- Stay alert for processes in acquired companies that you like, and introduce them as innovations into your own company.
- Personally perform regular follow-up to ensure that the acquisition really is performing even better than predicted by the valuation model.

———◇———

How adept are you at performing integrations? Do you have plans in place before the deal closes? Are you taking integration seriously, assigning top people to work on a full-time basis?

MANAGING YOUR PORTFOLIO

As helpful as structured processes are, you can't just drop them in place and assume your portfolio management will instantly become much more disciplined, strategic, and productive. There's an important ingredient we haven't yet considered: you and your leaders.

I've said it before: delegate as a leader, but don't abdicate. Here especially you want to take your oversight role seriously, applying the mindset of intellectual inquiry. When people in your team or organization come to you with possible deals to consider, push hard. If you hear that a company is in a good industry, seriously examine that. Who are the chief competitors? How profitable are they? Is the industry really as attractive as it seems? Regarding a prospective company's position in its industry, think hard about whether you might roll up multiple players in a fragmented industry to create a juggernaut. When Honeywell entered the gas detection business, there were no big players, but over an eight-year period we were able to acquire several companies, roll them up into a single Honeywell business, and become number one in the industry. We did the same in other industries, like barcode scanning, safety equipment, and digitally connected aircraft.

When considering potential acquisitions, keep a careful eye on risk as well as the impact on short-term results. Every quarter our businesses would bring me potential "elephants"—really big deals that, if consummated, would double Honeywell's size. I always backed away from these deals, fearful of the impact on our results if the deal didn't succeed as planned, and conscious as well that even if they did succeed, our short-term results would tank for quite a while due to the amortization we'd have to log.

Keeping risk foremost in your mind will also lead you to prioritize diversification. Having read former treasury secretary Robert Rubin's book *In an Uncertain World*, I became more inclined to consider the potential downsides of deals, even if the upside seemed great and far more likely to materialize. Low-probability events sometimes do occur, and you have to prepare, managing your portfolio so that you can stay flexible and respond to changing conditions.

When considering divestitures, do you rush to get the deal done, or do you spend time and effort readying your businesses for sale and cultivating potential buyers?

Do you personally give portfolio management the attention it deserves, or are you prone to abdicating leadership in this area to someone else?

POSTMORTEM ANALYSES

In the spring of 2018, I was packing my office in preparation for a move when I came across a letter I wrote back in the summer of 2011. Addressed to unknown future CEOs of Honeywell, this lengthy note offered my personal reflections on how to handle one of the most difficult situations a leader faces: steering an organization or team through bad economic times. I had felt compelled to write this letter because we had emerged from the Great Recession of 2008 in great shape, outpacing our peers and also Honeywell's historical performance during recessions. While the experience was still fresh, I wanted to capture my reflections on how we had done it, in the hopes that my successors would have an easier time dealing with similar situations in the future and wouldn't have to waste time learning what we'd learned.

If you haven't written such postmortem analyses (or "white papers," as we called them) for your organization, I strongly suggest it. Intellectual rigor is vital for organizations seeking to perform well today and tomorrow, and leaders are uniquely positioned to establish and maintain that rigor. By taking a couple of weekends to write up a memo on our handling of the Great Recession, I forced myself to recall key challenges we'd faced and to think carefully through our responses to them. Writing also allowed me to preserve institutional memory about best practices for our organization, and to push readers (in this case, directors and key executives) to think more deeply about recessions. I wrote these analyses when our organization had navigated a major challenge, learning in the process some lessons I felt it important to pass on.

---◇---

When you've successfully dealt with hard times, are you taking enough time to reflect on and record what you've learned for posterity?

LEADING THROUGH A RECESSION

As unpleasant as recessions are, you can use them to set the stage for future gains against your competition as long as you stay disciplined and maintain a balanced, short- and long-term approach. Two basic strategies become important here. First, prepare for recessions before they hit hard by cutting costs proactively while still keeping the company's long-term growth projects— including process redesigns and culture—intact. Second, even as you are cutting costs during the recession, anticipate what you can do to prepare for the recovery, which does come despite how gloomy conditions might currently look.

Managing short-term costs with the future in mind requires more effort on your part, and it requires *independent thinking*. Be quicker than most to prepare for recessions even when bad economic news hasn't yet hit completely. And in the depths of recession, stay calm while everyone else is panicking, remembering that good times will return and that your organization needs to be ready. You'll face passionate resistance from your staff, employees, and investors, but if you can hold your ground and stubbornly continue to manage for both the short and long term, these stakeholders will eventually thank you for it.

Recessions don't materialize out of nowhere. The signs and signals are out there, if you're alert to them.

———◇———

Do you heed early signs of bad economic times and take reasonable precautions, or are you content to listen to those who say, "This is no big deal"?

MAINTAINING YOUR TALENT BASE IN TOUGH TIMES

W hen leading through a recession, my fundamental goal was to ensure that customers didn't feel any impact from us, because without strong performance on behalf of customers, both investors and employees would suffer. Here, I would seek to cut costs enough to outperform our peers financially while also preserving our long-term industrial base. Some leaders feel badly about hurting employees with cost-cutting, so they avoid it, preferring to let investors bear the full brunt of declining sales. Cost-cutting is no doubt unpleasant, but leadership isn't always easy. Leaders have no good choices here—they must choose between the bad and the less-bad. The less-bad choices would allow us to outperform for our investors (even though stock prices were still down), keep employee pain to a minimum, and ready ourselves for a recovery.

Essential to your success during a recession is your decision to avoid layoffs unless they are permanent reductions, meaning that you would never rehire for the affected positions. Research shows that layoffs lead to lower levels of innovation, lower morale, poorer performance among remaining employees, diminished corporate reputations, and higher levels of customer defection. One study found that "after layoffs a majority of companies suffered declines in profitability."[9]

For most businesses, avoiding layoffs in a one- or two-year recession is common sense. Leaders need about six months to actually lay off employees once they have decided to do so. They have to identify which jobs they are going to eliminate and attend to all of the legalities. Once employees are gone, it takes six months of operations before you've recovered all the money you spent on severance and other elements of the layoffs. After that, maybe you'll get another six months of returns before the economic recovery begins. Once it does, you have to hire people back to handle increases in demand. If someone told you that it would take you six months to build a factory, six months to recover your investment, you'll get a return for six months, and then you'll shut it down, you'd never go for it because it would be ridiculous. Yet somehow leaders think it makes sense to do something similar with people.

———◇———

If you've thought about layoffs, do other alternatives exist? What about furloughs?

COMMON COST-CUTTING RESPONSES TO RECESSIONS

To help you think through the pros and cons of various cost-cutting ideas, I've compiled them in the following charts.

MATERIALS

Direct Material (material that goes directly into the manufacture of your products)

PROS
- If you can get price reductions from suppliers, terrific!

CONS
- It's tough to do, as most companies have contracts in place with suppliers. But you should definitely try.
- The impact of these cuts are delayed if you have to go through an inventory account.

Indirect Material/Services (payments to suppliers other than material that goes directly into the product)

PROS
- This is a great move to make because by reducing usage, you cut costs immediately.

CONS
- As long as these cuts don't impact customers, they're fair game.

EMPLOYEES

Temporary or Contract Employees

PROS
- These cuts lower your costs immediately. They work if you always maintain a small portion (10–20 percent) of your workforce as temporary/contract while observing applicable state/federal laws regarding classification.

CONS
- Make sure it doesn't affect customers.
- You have to keep an eye on legal classifications.

WAGES/SALARIES TO EMPLOYEES

Halt All Raises

PROS
- Avoids cost increase.

CONS
- May annoy some employees.

Layoffs

PROS
- These cuts affect only a small percent (10–20 percent) of the workforce.

CONS
- The financial returns aren't great.
- Your organization will accrue a big expense up front, with the potential for survivor guilt among remaining employees.
- Layoffs hurt your industrial base, compromising your ability to respond during the coming recovery.

Furloughs

PROS
- These are a lot less costly in financial terms.
- They preserve your industrial base for recovery.
- When recovery begins, employees feel better about it.

CONS
- Furloughs affect 100 percent of the workforce.
- They are more difficult to administer because laws vary among states and countries.

Benefits

PROS
- Employees don't feel the effects of benefits cuts immediately.
- The cost savings show up quickly in company financials.

CONS • Employees won't like benefits cuts, but they will recognize that such cuts are better than more furloughs or layoffs.

Depreciation/Amortization

PROS • As long as it doesn't affect customers, it's much less painful.

CONS • Difficult to impact because most of this is driven by past expenditures.

Bonuses

PROS • Employees see bonus reduction as essential, a sign that "we're all in it together."
• Cuts in bonuses have an immediate impact on financials.

CONS • Leaders feel like they're working harder than ever for a lot less. You can minimize resentment by finding a way to help leaders over time (for instance, by issuing bonuses in stock).

Direct Support to Customer (cooperative advertising, etc.)

PROS • Cuts in customer support have an immediate financial impact.

CONS • Customer impact cuts are a really bad idea, as they could cause customers to flee, hurting you over the long term.

---◇---

When times are tough, are you tempted to make cuts that impact your ability to deliver for customers or that undo the previous growth investments you've made?

KEEP SUPPLIER
RELATIONSHIPS STRONG

U p until now, I've focused on labor costs, but a strategy around materials will prove pivotal to your postrecession performance, even if it doesn't center around cost-cutting. One of the great difficulties businesses have as they exit recessions is that competitors are also ramping up production, so the supplies required for production become scarce up and down the supply chain.

Here's a scenario. When an airline, say, cuts its flight hours by 7 percent, leaders there reduce their orders for Honeywell spare parts by 25 percent and burn off their existing inventory to conserve cash. On the same logic, we'll reduce our own supply orders by 40 percent, and our suppliers will cut their own orders from vendors by 50 or 60 percent, compounding greatly the effect of a 7 percent decline in the end market. During recoveries, the opposite occurs: spikes in demand grow larger as you go down the supply chain. Yet suppliers one or two rungs down can't meet the demand when their orders double overnight—it takes time for them to rehire laid-off workers and access the materials they need. As a result, businesses can't grow as rapidly during a recovery as they otherwise might.

An economist I came across made a very simple prediction that struck me as both intuitive and correct: businesses would leave a recession in the manner they entered it. If you only saw a 2 or 3 percent decline in sales over the course of a year because you were a long-cycle business, you'll only see a 2 or 3 percent increase over a similar period during the recovery. If your short-cycle business tanked as the recession hit, with sales dropping 20 or 30 percent in the space of six months, then you could expect a 20 to 30 percent sales boost at some point as your business came back. By this logic, you could expect that your short-cycle businesses would see demand roaring back over a relatively short period of time. If your business couldn't access the supplies they needed, the recovery would become stalled, and your competitors will get the upper hand, or you will all struggle equally.

———————◇———————

What accommodations are you making with suppliers to ensure you can quickly ramp up to meet renewed demand?

WORK COLLABORATIVELY
WHEN MAKING BIG DECISIONS

When making big decisions, especially about cost-cutting and other sensitive issues, work collaboratively with other leaders on your team to make sure they're on board. Faced with actions that hurt employees, some of them will go into denial about the extent of the downturn. You can't dictate a solution and expect everyone's buy-in. Instead, put the conundrum you face, as well as your recommended actions, before your team members and let *them* come to their own conclusions. I like to divide a team into breakout groups for such deliberations, as I find this technique helps teams avoid the phenomenon of groupthink. Sometimes your team members will generate solutions you didn't think of—and that's great. Other times they'll agree with the cost-cutting measures you propose as the least-bad alternative. Because they had a chance to think through the issues for themselves, they can get behind what might ultimately prove to be a painful decision.

If you lead a large organization with hundreds or even thousands of leaders and managers, get all of them aligned with your cost-cutting strategy, not just your executive team. At Honeywell, we saw the difference leadership alignment made when we implemented furloughs in France. Under French law, employees had to volunteer to be furloughed. In some plants, we saw huge differences in the number of employees volunteering—one plant would have 5 percent in favor of furloughs, another 80 percent. When we examined what was happening, we found it all came down to plant managers, how they were portraying the furlough to people and how much trust their people had in them.

Communicating and being collaborative with other leaders in your organization will ensure that everyone has accurate information and better understands the issues the business is facing despite the grumbling that occurs among the workforce.

———————◇———————

Are you ruling by fiat when it comes to responding to the recession, or are you talking through dilemmas with other leaders and coming to difficult decisions together?

ALWAYS BE HONEST WITH YOUR EMPLOYEES

You should make it a priority to communicate openly and honestly with your employees. People must hear the truth about how the business is doing. If you present an overly rosy picture at the outset, you might have to go back and explain the situation yet again when sales have dried up further. At the same time, don't pretend you know for certain the status of the economy. Any predictions you make might come back to haunt you. When dealing with cuts or a challenging economy, acknowledge the pain people feel and help them understand why it's necessary.

In other words, provide hope—a very powerful human emotion. Whatever you do, let people know you're sacrificing too. Employees need to understand that the organization will treat people fairly during tough times. But as important as fairness is, please factor in the long-term consequences. Communicate to your employees that you are all in this together, and do what you can to ensure that you really are—but again, not at the expense of your long-term growth.

---◇---

Are you communicating openly and honestly enough with employees, helping them stay strong even when they're hurting?

MANAGE THE LEADERSHIP TRANSITION

No matter how diligent you've been at investing for the future while delivering profits today, your accomplishments always remain fragile, never more so than when it's time for you to step down. Will your successors know how to follow your disciplined approach to management? Will unexpected problems knock your successor off track, despite his or her best intentions? Will tensions or uncertainty arise inside the organization during the succession and transition process, distracting your successor? These are not simply academic questions. Bungled leadership transitions are common in business.

If you care about driving long- and short-term performance, plot the hand-off early, deploying the same kind of independent thinking you've mustered all along in other parts of the business. As your retirement nears, devote much more time and attention to shepherding your successor into your role than leaders often do. It's the best way to ensure that all the investments you've made will not only pay off, but they will also benefit the company and its people for years or even decades to come. No transition will ever go perfectly, but the goal should be a position your business can continue to build upon and thrive.

As tempting as it might be to procrastinate when it comes to succession, don't do it. The more you look at your business from both the short- and long-term perspectives, the more you realize that arranging for your successor isn't something outside the daily work of running your business—it's a vital part of your strategy and an outgrowth of the efforts you should be making all along to cultivate a strong leadership corps. If you don't plan successions well throughout your team or organization, chances are you won't do it well at the top level either.

───────◇───────

Are you thinking about who will succeed you, or have you pushed this analysis off to some nebulous future time?

What key qualities should your team's or organization's next leader have?

BE RELENTLESS

Rather than throw up your hands, make excuses, and assume that the way you've always done it is the only or best way, challenge your business to remake your organization and your culture top to bottom so that everyone can accomplish two conflicting things at the same time. You should follow through relentlessly to make sure you and your team actually execute the business strategy and plans and ensure that the teams have the tools they need to succeed. Turnaround won't be easy, so scrub accounting and business practices so you can see what's real. Being relentless doesn't mean being inflexible; you should invest in the future, but not at the expense of acceptable short-term returns, and grow while keeping fixed costs constant to generate flexibility.

Making specific changes will arouse considerable resistance within your organization. Even if some people liked a new idea or direction, they might still wonder how they can pull it off while continuing to perform their existing jobs. Of course, it's possible to take performance expectations too far. You don't need to be a twit in articulating these expectations, and you shouldn't ask people to do the truly impossible. But you do need to request the *seemingly* impossible, putting it to them in a kindly way and even with a sense of humor. On balance, though, organizations, people, and leaders would do well to be much more demanding of themselves than they are.

—————◇—————

What are some ways you can be more relentless as a leader and help your team?

How can you better handle pushback and resistance within your organization? What will be your biggest challenge when articulating expectations to your team?

1. "Global Leadership Forecast 2021," DDI World, accessed January 22, 2024, https://www.ddiworld.com/global-leadership-forecast-2021.

2. Lorena Castillo, "Employee Recognition Statistics [Fresh Research]," Gitnux, updated December 23, 2023, https://blog.gitnux.com/employee-recognition-statistics/.

3. "Measuring the Economic Impact of Short-Termism," McKinsey Global Institute, PDF, February 2017, 1, 2, 4, https://www.mckinsey.com/~/media/mckinsey/featured%20insights/long%20term%20capitalism/where%20companies%20with%20a%20long%20term%20view%20outperform%20their%20peers/mgi-measuring-the-economic-impact-of-short-termism.ashx.

4. Dennis Carey et al., "Why CEOs Should Push Back Against Short-Termism," *Harvard Business Review*, May 31, 2018, https://hbr.org/2018/05/why-ceos-should-push-back-against-short-termism.

5. "Lakeside Toxic Tombs," *Post-Standard* [Syracuse, NY], November 26, 2003; Amanda J. Crawford, "Honeywell Sued on Toxic Fuel Test Facility Releases at Issue for Arizona," *Arizona Republic*, July 10, 2004.

6. "Toyota Production System," Toyota, accessed October 8, 2019, https://www.toyota-global.com/company/vision_philosophy/toyota_production_system/origin_of_the_toyota_production_system.html.

7. Joe DeSarla, interview with the author, November 5, 2018.

8. William Oncken Jr. and Donald L. Wass, "Management Time: Who's Got the Monkey?" *Harvard Business Review*, November–December 1999 (reprint), https://hbr.org/1999/11/management-time-whos-got-the-monkey.

9. Sandra J. Sucher and Shalene Gupta, "Layoffs That Don't Break Your Company," *Harvard Business Review*, May–June 2018, https://hbr.org/2018/05/layoffs-that-dont-break-your-company.